www.capstonepub.com

Visit our website to find out more information about Heinemann-Raintree books.

To order:

☎ Phone 800-747-4992

💻 Visit www.capstonepub.com to browse our catalog and order online.

© 2013 Heinemann Library
an imprint of Capstone Global Library, LLC
Chicago, Illinois

Edited by Adam Miller, Andrew Farrow, and Laura Knowles
Designed by Steve Mead
Picture research by Mica Brančić
Original illustrations © Capstone Global Library Ltd 2013
Illustrations by HL Studios
Originated by Capstone Global Library Ltd
Printed and bound in China by CTPS

16 15 14 13 12
10 9 8 7 6 5 4 3 2 1

Library of Congress Cataloging-in-Publication Data
Spilsbury, Louise.
    Walruses / Louise Spilsbury.—1st ed.
        p. cm.—(Living in the wild: sea mammals)
    Includes bibliographical references and index.
    ISBN 978-1-4329-7066-6 (hb)—ISBN 978-1-4329-7073-4 (pb) 1.
Walrus—Juvenile literature. I. Title.
    QL737.P62S65 2013
    599.79'9—dc23   2012013348

Acknowledgments

We would like to thank the following for permission to reproduce photographs: Alamy pp. 14 (© Leo Keeler), 19 (© SuperStock/Mark Newman), 28 (Volvox Inc/© Tsuneo Nakamura); Corbis pp. 17 (© Paul Souders), 20 (© Paul Souders), 33 (epa/© Vincent Jannink),39 (© Wolfgang Kaehler); FLPA pp. 13 (Minden Pictures/Michio Hoshino), 16 (Bill Coster), Getty Images pp. 7 (National Geographic/Paul Nicklen), 11 (National Geographic/Paul Nicklen), 15 (National Geographic/Norbert Rosing), 23 (National Geographic/Paul Nicklen), 25 (Flickr/©2011 R Ungwiluk Jr/Rodney Ungwiluk, Jr. Photography), 26 (National Geographic/Paul Nicklen), 40 (SeaWorld/Bob Couey), 43 (National Geographic/Norbert Rosing); Nature Picture Library pp. 4 (© Steven Kazlowski), 12 (© Wild Wonders of Europe/Liodden), 22 (© Eric Baccega), 24 (© Bryan and Cherry Alexander), 30 (© Patricio Robles Gil), 35 (© Bryan and Cherry Alexander), 37 (© Steven Kazlowski); PhotoShot pp. 9 & 45 (© NHPA/John Shaw), 29 (© Juniors Tierbildarchiv), 31 (© NHPA/Jordi Bas Casas), 34 (© PictureNature/Peter Jones); Shutterstock pp. 6 right (© Alexander Kalina), 6 left (© Potapov Alexander); SuperStock p. 32 (© Minden Pictures).

Cover photograph of a walrus in Igloolik, Nunavut, Canada, reproduced with permission of Getty Images/Paul Nicklen.

Every effort has been made to contact copyright holders of any material reproduced in this book. Any omissions will be rectified in subsequent printings if notice is given to the publisher.

Disclaimer

Contents

Some words are shown in bold, **like this**. You can find out what they mean by looking in the glossary.

What Are Sea Mammals?

The huge, gray sea looks flat, calm, and empty, but then a huge animal drifts gently to the surface and sticks its head out of the water. It opens its mouth and makes a loud bellowing sound that can be heard far and wide! It is a walrus, one of the amazing sea **mammals** that live in seas all around the world.

A walrus is one type of sea mammal.

Sea mammals are animals that are dependent on the sea for food and that spend most of their time in or near the sea. Like land mammals, sea mammals give birth to live young, and the mothers produce milk for their babies. They also have backbones and hair on their bodies, although on many sea mammals this hair is barely visible.

Common features

There are different types of sea mammal. Some spend their whole lives in the water, such as whales and dolphins. Others, such as seals and sea lions, feed in the ocean but regularly **haul out** onto land to breed or rest. All sea mammals have features that help them to survive in the oceans. Like land mammals, they need to breathe air. They can hold their breath as they dive underwater in search of food, but they always come back to the surface to breathe. They also have thick fat (**blubber**) or fur to stay warm in cold water.

Type of sea mammal	How do they move?	Where do they live?
Whales and dolphins	use tail, fins, and flippers	These sea mammals live in water all the time.
Manatees and dugongs	use tail and flippers	
Seals, sea lions, and walruses	use flippers	These sea mammals spend some of their time in water and some on land.
Sea otters	use legs and tail	
Polar bears	use legs	

We can divide sea mammals into four groups. Seals, sea lions, and walruses are grouped together because they all have four **flippers**, blubber, and sensitive whiskers.

What Are Walruses?

Walruses are sea mammals that spend about two-thirds of their lives in the water. Walruses are large, powerful animals that are bigger than a small car! They have thick, wrinkly skin covered in short, thin, reddish-brown hair. Their square head is small compared to their body, with small red eyes, a short, flat snout, and a moustache of long, stiff whiskers. Their most noticeable features are their huge white tusks.

TERRIFIC TUSKS

A male walrus's tusks are two enormous **canine** teeth that can be up to 3 feet (1 meter) long. They are made of ivory, like an elephant's tusks, and keep growing throughout a walrus's life. Male tusks are straighter, thicker, and heavier than the female's.

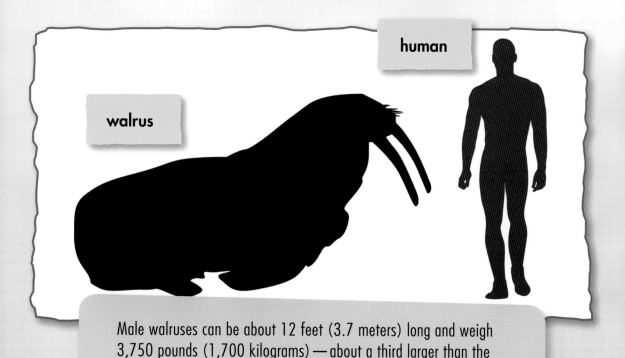

human

walrus

Male walruses can be about 12 feet (3.7 meters) long and weigh 3,750 pounds (1,700 kilograms) — about a third larger than the females. Male walruses are called bulls, and females are called cows.

Walrus evolution

Scientists are not sure how walruses **evolved**. The main theory is that they developed from a bear-like mammal that lived on the Pacific coast, hunting for food along the seashore around 30 million years ago. Gradually, these ancient creatures spent more time in the sea and developed **adaptations** that helped them swim and hunt in water. An adaptation is a feature that allows an animal to live in a particular place in a particular way. Animals develop adaptations as **species** evolve over thousands of years. These adaptations mean that, today, walruses can live in the sea and on land.

Millions of years ago, the **ancestors** of walruses lived on land. Today, walruses live in the sea, but they still come onto ice or land, too.

How Are Walruses Classified?

Scientists **classify** living things to identify them and to understand why and how they live where they do. *Classification* means grouping living things according to the characteristics or features they share.

Classification groups

The standard groups of the animal kingdom are phylum, class, order, family, genus, and species. Each group contains fewer and fewer members. So, there are fewer animals in the class Mammalia (mammals) than there are in the sub-phylum Vertebrata (vertebrates, or animals with backbones), and there are even fewer in the order Carnivora (meat-eating mammals). The walrus is the only living species in the Odobenidae family and *Odobenus* genus.

This pyramid shows how the walrus is classified. Animals are given a two-part Latin name, such as *Odobenus rosmarus*, to avoid confusion if they are known by different common names in different countries.

Kingdom:	Animalia	Animals
Phylum:	Chordata	Chordates
Sub-phylum:	Vertibrata	Animals with backbones
Class:	Mammalia	Mammals
Order:	Carnivora	Carnivorous
Family:	Odobenidae	
Genus:	*Odobenus*	
Species:		*Odobenus rosmarus*

Around 10 to 20 percent of the world's walruses are Atlantic walruses like this one.

Walrus differences

The walrus is in its own family, *Odobenidae*, because although it shares some features with seals and sea lions, it is unique. Walruses have no external ears like seals and they move on land like sea lions, but they are different in other, important ways. Walruses have tusks, and they can only breed with other walruses.

Subspecies

There are two subspecies of walruses: the Atlantic (*Odobenus rosmarus rosmarus*) and the Pacific (*Odobenus rosmarus divergens*). The two subspecies do not breed with each other, because they live in different parts of the world. Otherwise they are much the same, although the Pacific walrus is a bit bigger, with longer tusks and a wider skull.

Where Do Walruses Live?

Walruses live in and around the Arctic. This is the northernmost region on Earth, around the North Pole. It is an area with long, freezing-cold winters and short, warmer summers.

Atlantic walruses live in the Atlantic Ocean in coastal areas from northeastern Canada to Greenland and Svalbard (Norway), Franz Josef Land (Russia), the Barents Sea, and the Kara Sea. Pacific walruses live in the northern seas off Russia and Alaska, mainly in the Bering, Chukchi, and Laptev seas. The seawater around the North Pole is permanently frozen into a crust of ice known as **pack ice**. The cold seas around this pack ice are littered with slow-moving **ice floes**, which are platforms of floating ice.

North Pole

Bering Sea

Siberia

Area visible on map

Pacific Ocean

Chukchi Sea

Alaska (United States)

Laptev Sea

NORTH POLE

Franz Josef Land

Arctic Circle

RUSSIA

Arctic Ocean

CANADA

Svalbard

GREENLAND

Atlantic Ocean

This map shows where Pacific and Atlantic walruses live.

Walrus habitat

An animal's **habitat** is the environment where it lives—the place that provides it with everything it needs, including food, water, and shelter. Walruses may swim across deep water, but they spend most of their time in shallower water near coasts or near the edges of the pack ice or huge ice floes. They travel and feed in the sea and then haul out onto ice to rest and soak up the sun. When there is no ice nearby, they haul out onto small rocky islands.

Walruses usually live in icy seas where water is no deeper than about 260 feet (80 meters).

On the move

In the summer, when it gets warmer, the edges of the Arctic pack ice melt and the overall area of ice gets smaller. Walruses prefer to haul out onto ice because there they are safe from land **predators** and from being disturbed by people. So, most Pacific walruses follow the shrinking ice and **migrate** north to spend summer in the Chukchi Sea. It is mainly female and young walruses that travel north with the ice, and baby walruses are born on this migration. Less is known about the smaller Atlantic walruses, but they seem to stay in the same area all year round.

Walruses mainly migrate by swimming, but they may also ride on drifting ice floes.

Winter retreat

In the winter, temperatures drop, and the area of pack ice increases. The walruses that migrated north for summer return south again, staying along the edge of the pack ice as it expands. Several thousand Pacific walrus bulls remain in the south all year round. When the ice melts during the summer, they haul out on rocky islands instead.

MIKKEL VILLUM JENSEN

To study walrus migration, scientist Mikkel Villum Jensen shot **satellite** tags into walruses from a crossbow, a harpoon, and a gas-powered gun. The tags do not harm the walruses because of their thick skin and blubber. The tags sent signals to Jensen via satellites about the walruses' location, so he could figure out how far and where they go.

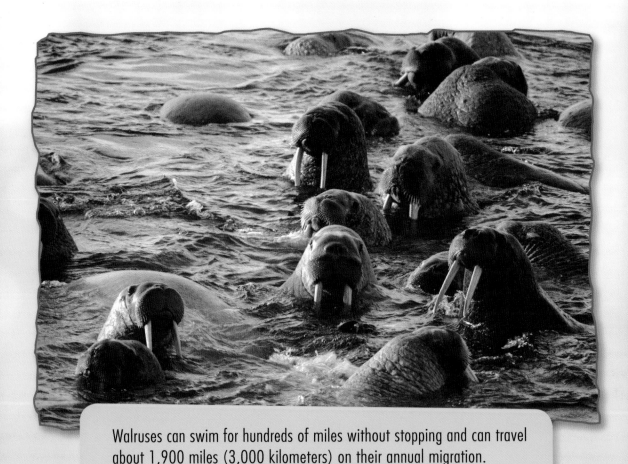

Walruses can swim for hundreds of miles without stopping and can travel about 1,900 miles (3,000 kilometers) on their annual migration.

What Adaptations Help Walruses Survive?

Arctic waters are among the coldest on Earth! Walruses have several adaptations that help them survive in their habitat of freezing water and floating ice.

Keeping warm

In water, animals lose body heat 25 times faster than they do on land. Like many other sea mammals, walruses have a layer of fat beneath their skin called blubber to keep them warm. Walrus blubber may be up to 4 inches (10 centimeters) thick. Walruses also tighten and narrow the blood vessels just beneath their skin, to reduce the amount of heat escaping from the blood into the air. When they do this, their skin looks very pale.

When walruses get hot in the sun, they expand the blood vessels under their skin so that heat leaves their body. This makes their skin look red.

LIVING IN THE WILD: SEA MAMMALS

WALRUSES

Louise Spilsbury

Heinemann
LIBRARY
Chicago, Illinois

Tackling ice

Ice is hard, smooth, and slippery, making it difficult to grip. Ice floes may be flat and constantly moving, so they are difficult to climb onto. A drop in temperature can freeze over channels in pack ice, stranding animals far from the water. A walrus's enormous tusks help it tackle these challenges. Walruses jab their tusks into ice to grip onto a floe and to haul their bulky bodies out of the water. They can also bash a hole through ice up to 8 inches (20 centimeters) thick with their head and enlarge it with their tusks to get into water.

The walrus's scientific name is Latin for "tooth-walking sea-horse," because it sometimes uses its long tusks to drag its body across land or ice.

Swimming and walking

Most animals live on either land or sea. Walruses have adaptations that allow them to move on both. A walrus's four flippers are shaped like short, wide paddles and are powered by large muscles. In the sea, the back flippers propel the walrus forward and the front flippers balance and steer. Walruses usually swim at over 4 miles per hour (about 7 kilometers per hour), but they can swim as fast as 22 miles per hour (35 kilometers per hour) when chased.

Like sea lions, walruses can rotate their back flippers to face forward and hold their front flippers at right angles. This allows them to walk on all fours on land. The skin on the soles of walrus flippers is hairless, thick, and rough, to help them to grip rock and ice.

Walruses lumber along awkwardly on land.

When walruses dive, their nostrils and tiny ear holes close tightly, and muscles in their throat close to stop water from getting into their lungs.

Diving

Walruses have special adaptations that help them to dive underwater for up to 10 minutes before coming up for air. Like many other sea mammals, walruses can store **oxygen** in their blood. Walruses can also store oxygen in their muscles to use when underwater. To conserve oxygen, the walrus can slow down its heartbeat while diving. It also diverts blood away from parts of the body that can function with less oxygen, such as the skin, to the heart and brain, where oxygen is needed most.

What Do Walruses Eat?

Walruses are carnivores (meat-eaters) that mostly eat animals living at the bottom of the ocean. They find most of their **prey** just below the surface of sand or gravel on the sea floor or just above it.

Shellfish suppers

Walruses mainly eat **mollusks**, such as clams and mussels, but they also eat snails, crabs, fish, and worms. Some walruses also feed on seals and even seabirds. Walruses are big animals with a big appetite. An adult walrus can eat more than 50 clams during a single seven-minute dive. In a day, it can eat 77 to 110 pounds (35 to 50 kilograms) of food!

Finding food

Walruses have fairly good eyesight underwater, but they usually hunt in deep or murky water, so they mainly use their long whiskers to locate prey. At the sea floor, they angle their heads toward the bottom and use their tusks like sleds to slide across the bottom. As they go along, their muzzle and whiskers feel for food. Then they swish their head from side to side to disturb the top layer of sediment. Sometimes they even squirt a jet of water at the sea floor to uncover a shellfish. Then they use their whiskers to bring the food into their mouth.

DIVING DEEP

Walruses usually eat prey that they find in water about 30 to 160 feet (10 to 50 meters) deep, although they can dive down to 820 feet (250 meters).

Walruses have about 450 whiskers, some of which are 12 inches (30 centimeters) long. They use their whiskers to find prey in the murky depths of the sea floor.

Dinner time

Most walruses dive and feed for 5 to 10 minutes at a time, with short breaks of a couple of minutes at the surface to breathe. They eat their prey where they catch it, and they can find and suck the meat from inside a shellfish in about six seconds. That is how an adult walrus can eat up to 6,000 clams a day.

VACUUM-PACKED FOOD?

Many shellfish can clamp their shells together very tightly. To feed, a walrus holds a mollusk in front of its strong thick lips and pumps its tongue up and down quickly. This creates an incredibly strong sucking force, and the walrus sucks the insides out of the shell like a powerful vacuum cleaner!

Walruses swallow worms and fish whole, but they suck the insides from mollusks such as clams and mussels.

Walrus food web

Animals eat other animals or plants and, in turn, may be eaten by other animals. This sequence is called a **food chain**. An ocean food chain starts with **algae**, such as seaweed, because they can make their own food using energy from sunlight. They are called producers. Animals are called consumers because they consume (eat) other animals or plants. Many connected food chains make up a **food web**. In this food web, for example, tiny, shrimp-like creatures called copepods eat microscopic algae that grows on the bottom of sea ice and floating phytoplankton. In turn, cod eat the copepods and krill that eat the phytoplankton. Then seals and walruses eat the cod.

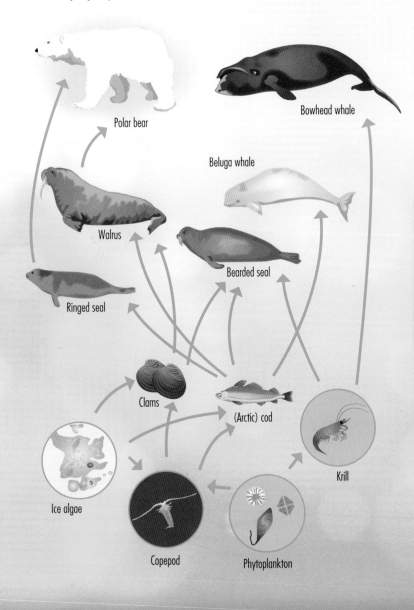

Polar bear

Bowhead whale

Beluga whale

Walrus

Bearded seal

Ringed seal

Clams

(Arctic) cod

Krill

Ice algae

Copepod

Phytoplankton

In a food web, the arrows go from the animal being eaten to the animal that eats it, to show the flow of energy.

What Is a Walrus's Life Cycle?

An animal's life cycle is the stages it goes through from birth to death. Sea mammals go through three main stages: birth, youth, and adulthood. Adulthood is when they reproduce and have young themselves.

Walrus displays

Male and female walruses usually live separately, but between December and March, bulls claim a **territory** near cows resting on ice. A territory is an area that an animal guards as its own. The strongest males growl, swim at, and even strike other bulls with their tusks to get the best spots near females on an ice floe. Then they perform displays in the water to attract a female. Bulls show off their tusks above water and make a variety of clicking and bell-like sounds underwater.

Bulls sometimes fight with tusks as they compete for territories and females.

Meeting and mating

When a bull impresses a cow with his displays, she leaves the ice and joins him in the water. At first they rub snouts with each other and dive together. Then they **mate** in the water. A cow mates only with one bull each season, while bulls mate with several different cows.

A female walrus usually hauls out onto the ice to give birth to a single baby, called a calf. Most calves are born as the females are migrating north.

Calves

Newborn walrus calves are gray-brown, with thick, short hair. They have short whiskers but no tusks yet. They are about 4 feet (1.2 meters) long and weigh about 132 pounds (60 kilograms). At two months old, calves **molt**. They shed their hair and it is replaced by a thinner, lighter coat. From then on, walruses molt every summer.

BUILT-IN FLOATS

Like other mammals, walrus cows feed their young on milk from their body. Females can float upright while their calves **suckle** upside down in the water! Walruses have pouches in their neck that they can fill with air to help them float.

Walrus calves suckle in the water and sometimes on ice or land. Walrus milk is 30 percent fat, which helps calves grow quickly.

Growing and learning

Calves can swim within hours of their birth and are strong swimmers by a month old. Calves follow their mothers on feeding trips, and mothers stop to let calves suckle when they need to. Tusks start to appear from about a year old. Walrus mothers teach their calves how to catch prey, how to haul out onto the ice using tusks, and where to find feeding spots. By six months old, calves also start to eat some meat, but they still stay with their mothers and suckle for at least two years—or longer if she has no other calves.

Type of sea mammal	Amount of time mothers suckle young
Hooded seal	4 days
Harp seal	12 days
Northern elephant seal	28 days
Sea lion	6 to 12 months
Walrus	2 or more years

Walruses suckle and care for their young longer than other sea mammals.

Walruses only have one baby every two or three years, so they make every effort to ensure it survives.

Care and protection

Walrus mothers are very protective of their calves. They try to leave their young on ice floes while they feed, rather than pack ice or land. This keeps calves safe from predators and from being accidentally crushed by lumbering males. If cows sense danger, they cover their calf with their front flippers. They fight off intruders with their tusks, and females sometimes guard each other's young.

WALRUS ADOPTION

Scientists studying walruses have discovered that females will adopt calves that lose their real mother. Orphaned calves are usually adopted by a female who does not have a calf of her own at the time. They may be cared for by an aunt or grandmother, or even by a female that is unrelated to them.

A walrus mother will often give her young calf a piggyback ride on her back.

Sea mammal		Life span
Leopard seal 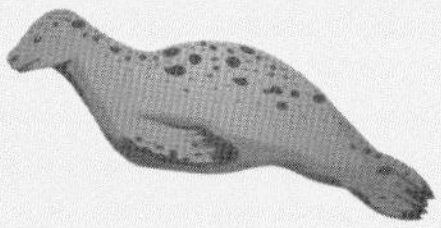		12–15 years
Sea otter 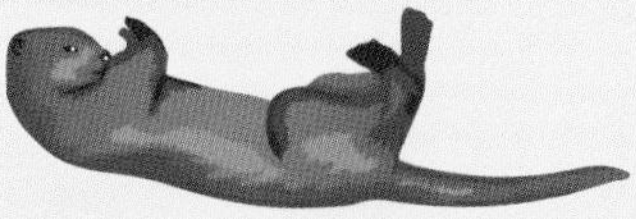		15–23 years
Harbor porpoise 		average 20 years
California sea lion 		up to 30 years
Walrus 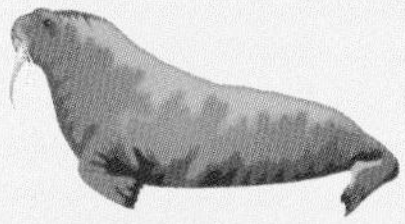		up to 40 years
Beluga whale 		35–50 years
Blue whale 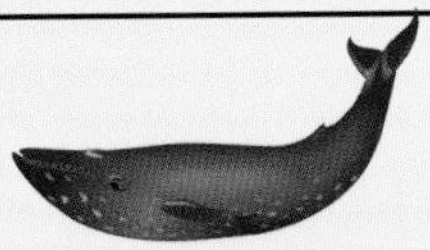		80–90 years

This chart shows the life span of some sea mammals in the wild.

Source: *National Geographic*

The cycle begins again...

Young walruses can take care of themselves after about two to three years. Young female walruses usually stay with their mother and other females, but males leave at that age. Females start to have young from about 9 or 10 years old, when they reach their maximum body size. After that, they usually have a calf every three years. Males could mate by 10 years old, but they cannot successfully compete with other males for a female until they reach their full adult size at 15 to 16 years of age. When young adult walruses have their own calves, the whole cycle begins again.

How Do Walruses Behave?

Walruses are very sociable animals and gather together in groups on pack ice or large ice floes when resting and migrating. These groups of walruses are known as **herds**.

When walruses haul out in a herd, they lie close to each other. Adults rest their heads on each others' backs, and calves often lie on top of the adults. Resting close together is a friendly thing to do, and it helps walruses to keep warm. Male walruses form separate herds from the females, and females with calves usually form separate groups, too. If they stay in the female herds, mothers with calves rest in the middle of the group or by the sea. Here the calves are better protected from predators.

There may be tens, hundreds, or even thousands of walruses in a herd.

Who's who in a herd?

In male herds, some bulls are more important than others. The longer the tusk and the bigger the walrus, the more important the walrus's rank in the group! For example, when a large male walrus comes out of the water, he looks for the best position at the haul out site. He often throws back his head and points his tusks at a smaller bull who is sitting where he wants to be. If that bull does not move, the big male strikes out with his tusks until he gets his way. Calves can be accidentally hurt or killed when huge bulls fight.

Walrus skin is strong, wrinkly, and about an inch (2 to 4 centimeters) thick. It acts as a sort of armor to protect bulls from some injuries when they fight other males.

A DAY IN THE LIFE OF A WALRUS

Within the **Arctic Circle**, the sun shines 24 hours a day in parts of the summer, and it is dark 24 hours a day during parts of the winter. Walruses spend much of their time feeding in deep, dark water, so they are not affected by changing patterns of light in the same way many other animals are. They swim, feed, rest, and sleep night and day.

SWIMMING AND FEEDING

Walruses are huge, but they eat small prey, so they spend a lot of time feeding to fill themselves up. They sometimes travel long distances to find good feeding spots. Feeding trips at sea can last up to several days, when they swim and dive almost continuously.

Walruses spend about two-thirds of their time swimming and feeding at sea, and they spend the other third on ice or land.

Walruses often sleep for many hours at a time.

RESTING

Walruses rest on ice or beaches between dives. They also haul out to rest and digest their meals for up to two days at a time after long feeding trips. They sleep on ice, land, or in the sea. Sleeping walruses fill their neck pouches with air to keep their heads above water. When walruses sleep, they snore!

JEROME SIEGEL

Scientist Jerome Siegel studied the sleep patterns of captive walruses. He discovered that they can swim and stay awake for up to 84 hours and sleep on land continuously for up to 19 hours. He also found that like whales, walruses rest one half of their brain at a time when sleeping, so that the other half remains alert to danger.

How Intelligent Are Walruses?

Walruses use sounds to do things such as find each other in the water and warn others about predators.

It is very difficult to measure and compare intelligence in animals, but many scientists think that one sign of intelligence is the way animals communicate. Walruses deliberately make different sounds to communicate different information.

Walrus communication

The walrus's flexible muzzle, large lips, and the fact it has vocal cords all allow it to make a variety of sounds above and below water. Males use their throat pouches to make a loud, bell-like sound during mating season, and they roar, cough, and snort to intimidate (scare off) others around them. Walruses also sing, clap, moan, whistle, and make knocking and clicking sounds.

COLLEEN REICHMUTH AND RON SCHUSTERMAN

Scientists Colleen Reichmuth and Ron Schusterman studied captive walruses being taught to create new sounds by their trainers, such as blowing raspberries! One walrus used a rubber toy as an instrument by pressing it against the glass of its pool and blowing air through it to make a trumpet sound. Two other walruses in the pool learned to do the same thing. "To use a tool to produce an innovative sound, and to learn about that behavior socially," Reichmuth said, "now that is impressive."

Captive walruses will respond to their keepers with different sounds and actions.

What Threats Do Walruses Face?

It is difficult to count walruses because they are spread over such a wide, remote area. Recent estimates are about 22,500 Atlantic walruses and 200,000 Pacific walruses. This may sound like a lot, but these numbers are falling because of the threats walruses face.

Polar bears hunt weak or dying adult walruses and chase herds of walruses that have hauled out onto land, catching calves that get separated from their mothers in the rush.

Predators

An adult walrus's strong tusks, huge size, and thick skin keep it safe from most predators. Young and dying walruses are preyed upon by killer whales in areas of open water and by polar bears on ice, but walruses are not a major part of either animal's diet. It is humans who pose a real threat to walrus numbers.

Hunting

From the 18th century, traders from the United States, Norway, Russia, Great Britain, Greenland, and Canada hunted walruses for meat, skin, ivory, oil, and other products. This resulted in the **extinction** of walruses in some areas and a severe reduction of numbers in others. This large-scale hunting was stopped in the mid-20th century, and numbers recovered in most areas.

Disturbance

Today, there are other threats. When oil and gas workers, tourists, and fishing boats visit their habitat, walruses may be scared away from useful haul-out spots. Herds also stampede back into the water from land when they hear planes and boats, often trampling calves to death. If young calves are separated from their mothers in the rush, they do not usually survive.

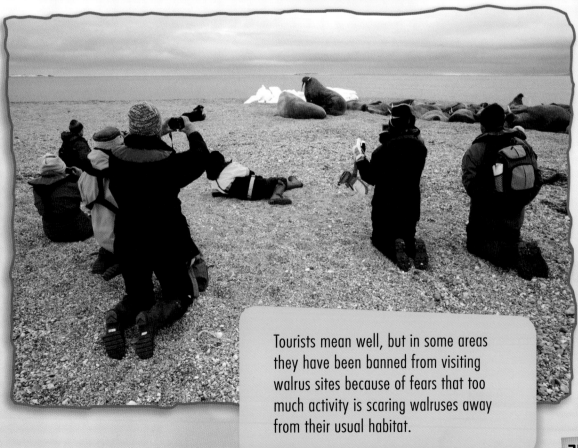

Tourists mean well, but in some areas they have been banned from visiting walrus sites because of fears that too much activity is scaring walruses away from their usual habitat.

Pollution

Pollution, such as oil, farm chemicals, or industrial waste, drifts to the Arctic in air or water. These things degrade very slowly in cold Arctic waters and enter the food chains. As larger animals such as walruses eat many smaller animals, the pollutants build up in their bodies. Large amounts of metals have been found in Atlantic and Pacific walruses, and large amounts of toxic chemicals have also been found in walruses that eat seals. When these things build up in a body, walruses and other animals are unable to have young and may get sick or die.

Animals at the top of a food chain get high levels of pollution in their bodies from eating many smaller animals containing pollution.

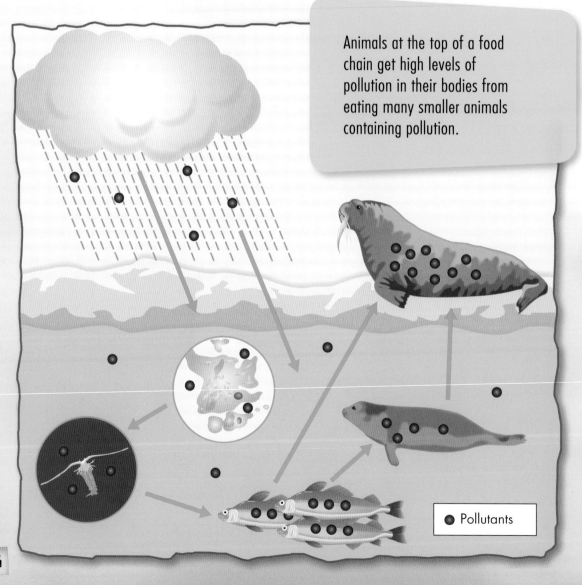

● Pollutants

Global warming

As temperatures rise due to **global warming**, ice floes in shallow waters where walruses feed are melting. Walruses have to dive from ice floes in deeper water to feed, so they get less food and there may be no clams there. When they rest on coastlines, they are farther from their food and closer to predators. When cows travel farther, calves left alone for longer may starve or get separated from their mothers.

INTERDEPENDENCE

Interdependence is the way in which living things in a habitat rely on each other for survival. As global warming makes the sea warmer, some small animals that thrive in cold waters may die out. This will affect other animals in the food web. If clam populations decline, there will be less food for walruses to eat.

Walruses rely on thick platforms of ice to rest on when tired, feed from, and travel on during their annual migration.

How Can People Help Walruses?

Many people are working to help walruses. Many organizations are calling for the walrus to be listed as an **endangered** animal. This would mean walruses would be protected under the U.S. Endangered Species Act against anything doing harm to them.

Protection

Walruses are currently protected by hunting restrictions. Today, only Inuit people and **native** Alaskans in some areas are allowed to hunt walruses, because it is central to their way of life. They are only allowed to take a limited number of walruses, and only if they use all or most of the animal for food and products for themselves.

Research

In order to create laws protecting walruses, governments need evidence that their numbers are decreasing. That is where research scientists can help. Walruses are spread over such a wide area that it is hard to count them, so scientists figure out herd numbers from sightings and pictures taken from ships and planes. Some planes have heat sensors that scan the ice to spot the walruses' warm bodies!

LORI POLASEK

In 2011, scientist Dr. Lori Polasek and her team set up cameras near beaches where walruses come ashore. The cameras took over 50,000 pictures without disturbing the walruses. Polasek wants to study mothers and their calves over several years, to see how safe they are on the island and if their population changes.

U.S. laws forbid trading in walrus animal parts, such as these walrus tusks. Some criminals kill walruses and then try to sell the animals' tusks over the Internet.

Zoos

Keeping some walruses in a well-kept zoo with properly trained staff can help people learn about these animals. This makes more people care about how human activities may have an impact on the walrus's survival. Watching walruses in zoos also allows scientists to study walruses in a way that would be difficult or impossible in the wild. In some zoos and parks, trained workers care for orphaned calves that have been abandoned by or separated from their mothers in the wild.

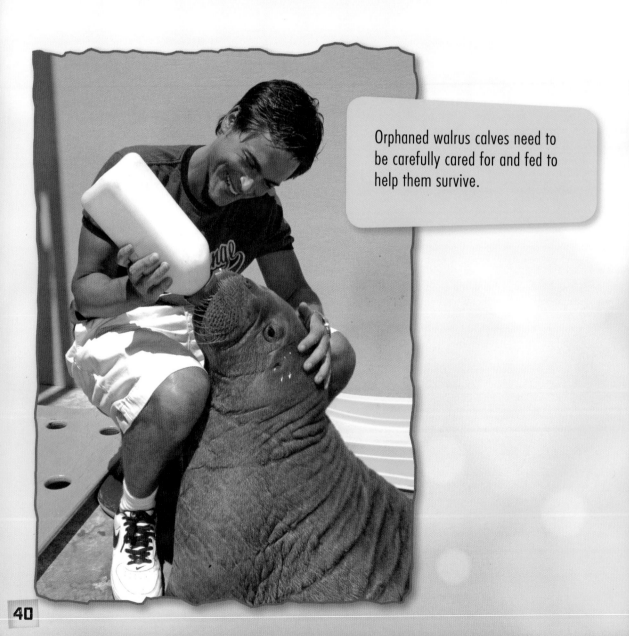

Orphaned walrus calves need to be carefully cared for and fed to help them survive.

What can you do?

Human activity such as burning coal to make electricity, using oil and gasoline, and cutting down rain forests and other forests are contributing to global warming. Individuals can help walruses by taking action to help reduce global warming and prevent more ice from melting. Here are some ways you can help:

- Share car trips, ride a bike, or take a bus to reduce oil use.

- Reuse a cloth bag instead of using plastic bags that are made with oil.

- Buy local foods and products that use less gasoline for deliveries.

- Write or print on paper on both sides.

- Try to buy products that do not use much packaging.

- Give unwanted gifts and clothes to a charity store. This reduces the number of new things made, which takes a lot of oil and electricity.

- Do not leave your television or computer on standby, as that still uses power.

- Switch lights off when you are not in the room.

- Use less hot water. It takes a lot of electricity to heat water.

- Turn the heating down and put a sweater on instead.

What Does the Future Hold for Walruses?

There is no immediate threat to the survival of the walrus, but experts believe the loss of sea ice due to global warming is a major threat to their future. The United States Geological Survey (USGS) has said that there is a serious risk that the walrus could be extinct by 2095 because of the rapid and widespread loss of summer sea ice. This reduces the ice platforms that walruses use and opens up their habitat to more disturbances. When areas of sea ice are reduced and other ice becomes thin enough to be broken through by ships, more people will travel to walrus habitats that were once too remote to reach.

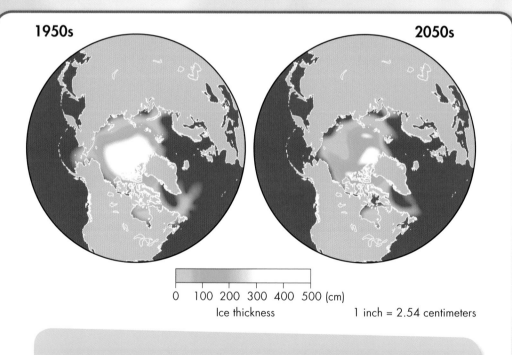

1950s   2050s

```
0   100 200 300 400 500 (cm)
        Ice thickness
```
1 inch = 2.54 centimeters

These maps show the average Arctic ice cover and thickness during the 1950s and how these might decline by the 2050s, if global warming continues at current rates.

Hope for the future

On a positive note, many organizations, individuals, and governments are working to protect walruses. This is very important, because the walrus is a keystone species. That means if it dies out, other species will die out, too. That is because as walruses rummage around on the sea floor, they stir up sediment and nutrients. Tiny living things in the sea need these to survive, and other animals in the food web need to eat the tiny living things! Rapid ice loss in the Arctic affects not only walruses, but Arctic people and other wildlife, too, so there is growing understanding of global warming and increasing pressure to tackle it.

Walruses are one of a kind! We need to protect these unique sea mammals so they continue enriching the natural world far into the future.

Species Profile

Species: Walrus

Latin name: *Odobenus rosmarus*

Length: Up to 12 feet (3.7 meters) for males

Weight: Up to 3,700 pounds (1,700 kilograms) for males

Habitat: Arctic and subarctic oceans, rocky and icy shores

Diet: Invertebrates such as clams and crabs, and some fish

Life expectancy in the wild: Up to 40 years

Number of young: One infant is born after around 15 months of pregnancy. Females will give birth about every three years.

mouth—large lips used to feel for prey on sea floor

ear holes

whiskers—used to feel along seabed and touch prey

small, red eyes

tail—small and hidden inside folds of skin

tusks—males and females have two long, ivory tusks

front flippers—used for steering in water and walking on land

skin—very thick, with blubber beneath for warmth

back flippers—used for swimming in the water and walking on land

Glossary

adaptation body part or behavior of a living thing that helps it survive in a particular habitat

algae plant-like living thing that grows on land and in the sea

ancestor early type of animal or plant from which others have evolved

Arctic Circle area consisting of the ice-covered Arctic Ocean and surrounding land, including Greenland and the northern parts of Alaska, Canada, Norway, and Russia

blubber layer of fat between the skin and muscle of most sea mammals

canine type of long, pointed tooth that a carnivore has

classify group living things together by their similarities and differences

endangered describes a species that is in danger of dying out

evolve change gradually over time

extinction when all animals in a species die out, we say that species is extinct

flipper broad, flat limb supported by bones and adapted for swimming

food chain sequence in which one creature eats another, which eats another, and so on

food web network of intertwined food chains

global warming rise in temperature of Earth's atmosphere, probably caused by human activities

habitat natural environment of a living thing

haul out leave the water to get on land

herd group of certain large animals that associate together

ice floe large piece of floating ice

interdependence way that all of the living things in a habitat and the habitat itself rely on each other for survival

mammal animal that has fur or hair, gives birth to live young, and feeds its young on milk from the mother

mate come together to reproduce or have young

migrate move from one region to another

mollusk member of a group of animals that includes mussels, clams, oysters, snails, and squid

molt shed old fur and grow a new layer of fur

native person born in that place

oxygen gas in the air that animals need to breathe

pack ice huge, dense area of ice formed from seawater in Earth's polar regions

pollution something that gets into the environment that has harmful or poisonous effects

predator animal that eats other animals

prey animal eaten by another animal

satellite machine in space that receives and transmits from and to Earth

species group of similar living things that can mate with each other

suckle take milk from a mother's body

territory area of land than an animal claims as its own

Find Out More

Books

Read, Tracy C. *Exploring the World of Seals and Walruses*. Buffalo, N.Y.: Firefly, 2011.

Rebman, Renee C. *Walruses* (Animals, Animals). New York: Marshall Cavendish Benchmark, 2012.

Stefoff, Rebecca. *Sea Mammals* (Family Trees). New York: Marshall Cavendish Children's Books, 2009.

Web sites

www.defenders.org/walrus/basic-facts
This web site offers more facts about walruses as well as idea for how you can help save the walrus.

kids.nationalgeographic.com/kids/animals/creaturefeature/walruses
This site has information, maps, and video clips about walruses.

www.seaworld.org/animal-info/info-books/walrus/index.htm
You will find lots of information about walruses on Seaworld's web site.

Organizations to contact

Endangered Species International
www.endangeredspeciesinternational.org/index.php
This organization focuses on saving endangered animals around the world.

WWF
www.worldwildlife.org
WWF works to protect animals and nature and needs your help! Take a look at its web site and see what you can do.

Index